BELOW PAR

© 1992 PAWS, INCORPORATED
All rights reserved.

(Garfield Comic Strips: © 1990, 1991, 1992 United Feature Syndicate, Inc.)

First published by Ravette Publishing 1992

This book is sold subject to the condition that it shall not, by way of trade or otherwise, be lent, re-sold, hired out or otherwise circulated without the publisher's prior consent in any form of binding or cover other than that in which it is published and without a similar condition including this condition being imposed on the subsequent purchaser.

JIM DAVIS

Printed and bound for
the Publishers by
Cox & Wyman Ltd.,
Reading, Berkshire
by arrangement with
RAVETTE PUBLISHING LTD.,
3 Glenside Estate,
Star Road,
Partridge Green,
West Sussex RH13 8RA

ISBN 1 85304 411 8

RAVETTE PUBLISHING

First published by Ravette Publishing 2002

Printed and bound in Great Britain
for Ravette Publishing Limited,
Unit 3, Tristar Centre,
Star Road, Partridge Green,
West Sussex RH13 8RA

by Cox & Wyman Ltd, Reading, Berkshire

ISBN: 1 84161 152 2

MRS. FEENEY, I MAY HAVE A CLUE TO THE FATE OF "MISTER SWEETYWINGS"

JIM DAVIS 4·16

www.garfield.com

ELLEN, KNOW WHAT I'D LIKE TO DO?

RUN OVER THERE AND SWEEP YOU OFF YOUR FEET!

JPM DAVPS 5-12

SHE'S NAILING HERSELF TO THE FLOOR

OUCH

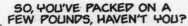

OTHER GARFIELD BOOKS AVAILABLE

Pocket Books	Price	ISBN
Bon Appetit	£3.50	1 84161 038 0
Byte Me	£3.50	1 84161 009 7
Double Trouble	£3.50	1 84161 008 9
Eat My Dust	£3.50	1 84161 098 4
Fun in the Sun	£3.50	1 84161 097 6
The Gladiator	£3.50	1 85304 941 7
Gooooooal!	£3.50	1 84161 037 2
Great Impressions	£3.50	1 85304 191 2
Hangs On	£2.99	1 85304 784 8
In Training	£3.50	1 85304 785 6
The Irresistible	£3.50	1 85304 940 9
Let's Party	£3.50	1 85304 906 9
Light Of My Life	£3.50	1 85304 353 2
On The Right Track	£3.50	1 85304 907 7
Pick Of The Bunch	£2.99	1 85304 258 7
Says It With Flowers	£2.99	1 85304 316 8
Shove At First Sight	£3.50	1 85304 990 5
To Eat, Or Not To Eat?	£3.50	1 85304 991 3
Wave Rebel	£3.50	1 85304 317 6
With Love From Me To You	£3.50	1 85304 392 3

new title available February 2003

No. 45 – Pop Star	£3.50	1 84161 151 4

Theme Books		
Guide to Behaving Badly	£4.50	1 85304 892 5
Guide to Cat Napping	£4.50	1 84161 087 9
Guide to Coffee Mornings	£4.50	1 84161 086 0
Guide to Creatures Great & Small	£3.99	1 85304 998 0
Guide to Healthy Living	£3.99	1 85304 972 7
Guide to Insults	£3.99	1 85304 895 X
Guide to Pigging Out	£4.50	1 85304 893 3
Guide to Romance	£3.99	1 85304 894 1
Guide to The Seasons	£3.99	1 85304 999 9
Guide to Successful Living	£3.99	1 85304 973 5

new series now available

2-in-1 Theme Books		
The Gruesome Twosome	£6.99	1 84161 143 3
Out For The Couch	£6.99	1 84161 144 1

Classics	Price	ISBN
Volume One	£5.99	1 85304 970 0
Volume Two	£5.99	1 85304 971 9
Volume Three	£5.99	1 85304 996 4
Volume Four	£5.99	1 85304 997 2
Volume Five	£5.99	1 84161 022 4
Volume Six	£5.99	1 84161 023 2
Volume Seven	£5.99	1 84161 088 7
Volume Eight	£5.99	1 84161 089 5

new titles now available

Volume Nine	£5.99	1 84161 149 2
Volume Ten	£5.99	1 84161 150 6

new series now available

Little Books

Food 'n' Fitness	£2.50	1 84161 145 X
Laughs	£2.50	1 84161 146 8
Love 'n' Stuff	£2.50	1 84161 147 6
Wit 'n' Wisdom	£2.50	1 84161 148 4

Miscellaneous

new title available September 2002

Treasury 3	£9.99	1 84161 142 5
Treasury 2	£9.99	1 84161 042 9
Address Book (indexed) inc vat	£4.99	1 85304 904 2
21st Birthday Celebration Book	£9.99	1 85304 995 6

All Garfield books are available at your local bookshop or from the publisher at the address below. Just tick the titles required and send the form with your payment to:-

RAVETTE PUBLISHING
Unit 3, Tristar Centre, Star Road, Partridge Green, West Sussex RH13 8RA

Prices and availability are subject to change without notice.
Please enclose a cheque or postal order made payable to **Ravette Publishing** to the value of the cover price of the book and allow the following for postage and packing:

60p for the first book + 30p for each additional book
except *Garfield Treasuries* and *21st Birthday Celebration Book* . . . when please add £3.00 per copy for p&p

Name ....

Address ....

....

....